Naomi Sheldon and Debl

GOOD GIRL

Written and performed
by Naomi Sheldon

Published by Playdead Press 2018

A CIP catalogue record for this book is available from the British Library.

ISBN 978-1-910067-61-1

Playdead Press
www.playdeadpress.com

Good Girl premiered in association with the Old Red Lion Theatre and Bruised Sky Productions on 3rd August 2017 at Just the Tonic at the Edinburgh Fringe.

The show previewed at VAULT festival on 28th Feb 2018 before transferring to Trafalgar Studios 2 on 5th March 2018.

CAST

Naomi Sheldon | GOOD GIRL

CREATIVE TEAM

Writer | **Naomi Sheldon**

Director & Dramaturg | **Matt Peover**

Designer | **Alison Neighbour**

Producer | **Debbie Hicks**

Stage Manager | **Anna Lavender**

PR | **Flick Morris**

Marketing Consultant | **Beth Nichols**

Photography | **Felicity Crawshaw**

Graphic Designer | **Rebecca Pitt**

Naomi Sheldon | GOOD GIRL

Naomi trained at LAMDA. Theatre and comedy includes: *The canon: a literary sketch show* (Underbelly); *Worlds* (VAULT); *Partners in Crime* (Queen's Theatre Hornchurch); *Don't Waste Your Bullets on the Dead* (VAULT); *Peter Pan Goes Wrong* (UK No.1 tour); *The Pride* (Trafalgar Studios and on tour); *A Midsummer Night's Dream* (Royal and Derngate); *Merry Wives of Windsor* and *The Mouse and His Child* (both RSC); *Sex with a Stranger* (Trafalgar Studios); *Wind in the Willows* (The Watermill); *Reclining Nude with Stockings* (Arcola); *The Emperor Jones* (National Theatre) TV includes: *Red Dwarf, Great War Diaries, Doctors, The Hour, The Mystery of Edwin Drood, Ashes to Ashes.* Radio includes: *Incredibly Guilty* (Radio 4). Film includes: *Cla'am, Hi-Lo Joe.* Naomi is also an improviser and trained with The Free Association. For her debut play *Good Girl,* Naomi was awarded a Pick of the Fringe award (Voice) and is currently developing it for television.

Matt Peover | Director

Comedy includes: *Mr Swallow: Dracula and Mr Swallow: Houdini*, Henry Paker and Mike Wozniak: *The Golden Lizard*, Jayde Adams' *Jayded* (Pleasance Edinburgh and Soho Theatre), Nick Helm: *This Means War* (Pleasance Edinburgh and Bloomsbury Theatre), Nina Conti: *In Therapy* (Pleasance Edinburgh), Holly Burn: *I am Kirsty K and I am Special*, *The Fitzrovia Radio Hour* (Guilded Balloon), Letluce: *Live Bait, Show Pony* and *Sea Men - A Navel Tale* (Just the Tonic and Soho Theatre). Theatre includes: *Powder Monkey* (Manchester Royal Exchange), *The Musician* (Belfast Festival), *Patching Havoc* (Theatre 503), *Endgame, Cowboy Mouth, Crave, Feeding Time* with Liquid Theatre (BAC), *Hamlet* (Natural Perspectives), *The Liberation of Colette Simple* (Jackson's

Lane), *The Exquisite Corpse* (Southwark Playhouse), *Jitterbug Blitz* (Lyric Hammersmith). Screen comedy includes: *Mr Swallow's Valentine* (Sky) and the short films *Pick Your Own* and *A Very Serious Game* (See Here Pictures).

Alison Neighbour | Designer

Alison trained at RADA. Recent work includes: *The Little Prince* (Playground Theatre); *The Girl With Incredibly Long Hair* (Wales Millennium Centre); *Hanging in the Balance* (mac, Birmingham); *Constellations & A Peter Rabbit Tale* (Singapore Repertory Theatre); *Ross & Rachel* (UK tour); *Spine* (UK Tour); *The Curtain* (Young Vic); *De-Railed* (HOME, Manchester); *Phenomenal People* (Fuel, UK Tour); *Crazy Gary's Mobile Disco* (Chapter Arts Centre & Wales tour); *I Told You This Would Happen* (ARC, Stockton & UK tour); *Lost in the Neuron Forest* (Wales Millennium Centre & UK tour); *The Eyes Have It* (Imagine Watford Festival); *Followers* (Southwark Playhouse); *Used Blood Junkyard* (Arcola); *Square Bubble* (InTransit & National Theatre)

Alison's design work was exhibited at World Stage Design 2013 and Make/Believe 2015. Alison is also co-founder of Bread & Goose, a company who create site responsive journeys through places and communities, and she is an Associate Designer at the Marlowe Theatre, Canterbury.

Debbie Hicks | Producer

Debbie is a theatre producer and manager working independently to deliver exceptional theatre and events in the West End, off West End, and on tour in the United Kingdom and internationally. She trained as an apprentice under the Stage One initiative for new producers, and now collaborates with a host of both emerging and established theatre makers.

Debbie is also a postgraduate student of the University of Oxford and a member of the Society for Theatre Research.

Credits as Producer: *Good Girl* (Vault Festival & West End); *The Retreat* (Park Theatre); *Cosmo* (in development); *North of the Sunset: Thelonious Monk & The Jazz Baroness* (in development); five-star sell-out kids show *Shakespearience* (UK Tour); Ray Cooney's Olivier award-winning *Out Of Order* (UK Tour); *Million Dollar Quartet* (International Tour); *Dinner With Friends* (Park Theatre), and Tom Basden's *Holes* (Arcola)

Credits as Manager: *Five Guys Named Moe* (Underbelly Marble Arch); *Brokeback Mountain* (in development); Joe Orton's *Loot* (Park Theatre); *The Boys In The Band* (Park Theatre, UK Tour & West End); *Babe, the Sheep-Pig* (UK Tour); *Raising Martha* (Park Theatre); *Impossible* (West End & International Tours); *Let It Be* (West End & International Tours), and *Neville's Island* (West End).

Anna Lavender | Stage Manager
Anna trained in Stage Management at Guildhall School of Music and Drama where she stage managed opera and a range of dramas. She has worked extensively in fringe theatre, in London, Edinburgh and around the UK.

Anna has a particular interest in new writing and comedy, leading her to work with companies such as Aine Flanagan productions, Berk's Nest and Fight in the Dog, where she stage managed their production of *Ricky Whittington and His Cat* at the New Diorama Theatre. She also works on the West End as an ASM dep for *Les Misérables*.

Naomi would like to thank the following individuals without whom this production would not have been possible: *Clive Judd* and *Gus Miller, Martin Murphy, Charlotte Josephine, Daniel Goldman, Alex* and *Sara Ratcliffe, Felicity Crawshaw, Flick Morris Michael Barfoot, Ray Cooney, James Seabright* and *Andrew Treagus.*

With special thanks to: *Greg Dyke, Dan Brodie, Henry Paker, Amy Beth-Hayes, Melanie Mehta, Amita Sehgal, Jane Austin, Trevor Sheldon* and *Michael Peover.*

For my husband, and all the good girls

CHARACTER:

GOOD GIRL | any age, any accent. She should play the other parts.

Music tracks in brackets are suggestions.

Lines in italics within brackets are stage directions.

Spaces between speech indicate a change of energy or location.

There was a little girl
Who had a little curl
right in the middle of her forehead.
When she was good, she was very, very good
and when she was bad she was horrid.

Henry Wadsworth Longfellow

"Some things are hard to write about. After something happens to you, you go to write it down, and either you over dramatize it, or underplay it, exaggerate the wrong parts or ignore the important ones. At any rate, you never write it quite the way you want to."

Sylvia Plath

The Unabridged Journals of Sylvia Plath

GOOD GIRL: 1995. I am 10 years old and about to make history at the swimming gala.

People are screaming. This is one intense mixed medley relay race. *The noise in here.* Laura is shouting so hard her face has gone purple. *My goggles are steaming up.* Sarah's body is making its way towards me with her bizarre take on butterfly. The technique doesn't make any sense but it works. We are two strokes ahead of the competition and gaining. Oh my god, we might actually win this! But there's one lap left… and it's mine. *The sound is deafening.* One tap on the side of the pool and it's all down to me. Zoe is giving me a double thumbs up. Coach is looking at me. I've been avoiding her ever since she told me off for kissing Jonny Garner in the cloakroom, even though it was only for a dare.

Why isn't he in trouble too?

COACH: He's just a young man stretching his wings, you should know better.

GOOD GIRL: Wait, what?

COACH: I shouldn't say this, but you're the sort of girl that'll use up our NHS resources, if you know what I mean.

GOOD GIRL: I don't know what she means.

I'm sorry?

COACH: If you're really sorry you'll sign up to do the last lap of the relay race.

GOOD GIRL: No one wants to do the last lap.

Coach is mouthing something at me. Good girl. Ooo. It feels nice. Makes me feel special. I mouth back 'thank you'. Don't know why I did that, I feel, yeah, I feel… angry. *Tap.* I launch into the air, flying momentarily *THE NOISE* and cut into the water. Smash smash glide. Turn my head to breathe, hear my name 'GG, GG' but this ball of rage is building in my belly. Smash smash glide. Pressing up against my insides. Smash smash glide. If I don't do something, I'm going to burst in a minute. Smash smash glide. I'll end up shouting, screaming 'it's not fair why isn't Jonny Garner doing the last bloody lap' and explode all over the pool. So I do the only thing I can do to avoid an outburst. Right here in the middle of the pool, in the middle of the under 11s inter-school South Yorkshire mixed medley relay race semi-final, I dive to the bottom of the pool. *Exhale.* The screaming turns to a warm rumble. *Exhale.* I reach the bottom of the pool and sit cross-legged, like a

Buddha. It's peaceful. I take a moment to contemplate. One, two, three bodies zoom overhead. Well I can't go up now. The last bubbles leave my nose and rush upwards. I need air. My body is convulsing, asking me to let it inhale. I can't stay here but I can't go up either. I'm trapped. I haven't the strength to resist the arms that pull me up through the water.

GIRLS: It was cramp right?

GOOD GIRL: I look at the girls' faces. They look frightened. I want to tell them about the *(the exploding)* – but what if none of them, *(suddenly realising)* what if no-one in the whole world feels this… much.

(beat)

Yeah, yeah it was cramp.

(Le Freak by Chic)

(Gets on her bike and cycles) I swing my bike over the front gate, shout BYE to dad, and peddle into the drizzle to Laura's house. The problem with Sheffield is it's very hilly. Ooh nice bunch of flowers – for the postman who got shot down our street. Don't know what he'd done. Why would you shoot a postman? He's just the messenger. Everyone knows you

don't do that. I used to hate this dirty grey city when we first moved here from London. But I've fallen in love. With my girls.

(Gets off bike)

LAURA: Laura, slender, long delicate fingers. I don't dot my I's, I put love hearts over them.

SARAH: Sarah, short and bendy like a gymnast. Red of face and hand. Terrible eczema. I leave puffy clouds of skin in the sunlight.

ZOE: Zoe. Literally a head and shoulders above everyone. But don't want to be so I've got a little stoop. Long chestnut hair down to me bum though so... *(this makes her special)*

GOOD GIRL: She leant down and kissed me on the lips once. I love her.

Emergency conference at Laura's. Thick pink carpet, excellent snacks and her own telephone. I know. Like an actual grown up lady boss.

The agenda:

LAURA: Unexplained Tingling of the Fanny. What is it? Do you get it? And is there a name for it?

GOOD GIRL: She hands around a plate of party rings.

SARAH: Yes, I do, I get that.

GOOD GIRL:	Sarah does a perfect handstand, springs into a front roll and picks up a party ring.
SARAH:	Do you Zoe? *(eats party rings and scratches arm)*
ZOE:	Yeah I do. I tingle. *(beat)* Sarah stop scratching your eczema, it's disgusting.
LAURA:	Yeah, you're shedding on my carpet.
SARAH:	Sorry. *(mouth full and trying not to scratch)*
GOOD GIRL:	I fiddle with my new digital bubble watch ring. I'm nervous. I get that when I watch films. Like *Ghost.*
ZOE:	Ooo yeah. That'd do it.
SARAH:	Oh, totally.
LAURA:	Mmm.
GOOD GIRL:	We concur that certain things inspire powerful sensations down below. A gorgeous tingling followed by a sort of heaviness? This could be brought on by Michael Jackson singing 'Annie are you OK?' for example. We all want to be Annie and we are more than OK. And also by receiving very delicate stroking of the arms from one another.
ZOE:	So what is it?

SARAH: And is there a name for it?

LAURA: We need to invent a secret one.

GOOD GIRL: A word pops into my head out of the blue.

A Swayze?!

LAURA: A Sw – a Swayze?

ZOE: Oh yeah, him from Ghost.

GOOD GIRL: Patrick Swayze hasn't died yet so it's not weird. His name isn't tinged with that same sadness as it is today.

It's perfect. We adopt it with immediate effect.

(GG is in the classroom writing)

In history, during a lesson about Henry VIII Sarah turns around to me and whispers

SARAH: I just Swayzed really hard.

GOOD GIRL: The intrigue, the frothy ruffs, those little dogs that are always in the corner of the portraits. The Tudor era is particularly ripe for a Swayze.

(Still in class they whisper)

ZOE: Mr. Melgate just asked me if I've started my period *again*.

GOOD GIRL: Mr. Melgate is always asking us girls this.

And have you?

ZOE: No.

LAURA: As if I'd tell him anyway.

SARAH: I heard he was having an affair with one of the mums.

LAURA: Who's mum?

SARAH: I don't know it could be anyone's.

LAURA: Mmm. It's probably yours.

GOOD GIRL: Mr Melgate has decided that to improve school behaviour on trips the girls must hold hands with the boys *even though we are way too old for this.* I always get partnered with – Nadeem Sadik.

NADEEM: In Batman yeah would you be a baddy or a goody?

GOOD GIRL: Nadeem likes to swing sticks while asking me life's big questions.

A baddy?

I want to be a goody. I want to be a goody so bad but I know that's not the cool answer.

NADEEM: A baddy? Yeah me too.

GOOD GIRL: I have this vivid dream where Nadeem kisses me and even though I quite like it I start to pull away, but our lips are stuck together and the more I move away the more our lips stretch until they are one long lippy string like pulled chewing gum and I wake up. And I'm still having a Swayze.

(Smooth Criminal by Michael Jackson)

Sleepovers at Zoe's are the best because there're always potato waffles in the freezer. We discover whilst lying in each other's arms and watching *Casper* for the fifth time that we all have our own smell. Which is weird given that we all wear White Musk by the Body Shop. Laura is

LAURA: Lemony? Oh I like that.

GOOD GIRL: Sarah

SARAH: Soapy? Probably because of all the E45.

GOOD GIRL: Zoe

ZOE: Milky?!

GOOD GIRL: And me

Spicy? What do you mean spicy, what like a curry?

LAURA: No not a curry, just like spices.

SARAH: Like a warm smell.

ZOE: It's nice GG it's nice! I mean I'm milk for God's sake. What, like a cup of tea?

GOOD GIRL: I wrap myself around Zoe, lay my head on her chest and we become spicy milk.

Us four, us band of girls, we speak too fast, laugh too easily, too loudly and have so many secrets we need each other just to share everything we've been storing up the whole of our lives.

Well not everything. I don't share everything.

I don't share that I've got this problem with my skin. Not like a rash or anything. It's that it doesn't do its job properly... of keeping me in. I keep, spilling / no, it's more like yeah seeping, yeah.

I keep seeping out of myself.

It can be quite nice. It can be amazing. Wrapped in my girls' arms I inhale them and melt through fish net skin and it's delicious. Like sinking into a hot bath. The problem is when I feel too much in here, the edges of me can't contain whatever this is inside, this ball of feeling. It's violent and it's ugly and it's embarrassing and it grows until it's pressing up against the insides of my skin and I feel like I'm going to tear open, and I guess I, yeah, I feel like I'm going to… disappear.

I mean will I evaporate? One of these days am I going to evaporate? Right here?

I don't think I have solid edges.

Casper eats a bomb and it explodes in his stomach. I hold Zoe tight, inhale her shampoo.

(The Way you Make me Feel by Michael Jackson)

I walk into school with the title Spice in my head and it makes me peppery.

I see Greg Morris in the playground, but he gives me a funny look and with no warning whatsoever, I kick him in the balls.

GREG: Why?!

GOOD GIRL: I don't know!

In science, Nicholas Richardson refuses to pass me the Bunsen burner, he ignores me so I… kick him in the balls.

NICHOLAS: What d'ya do that for?!

GOOD GIRL: nyuh?! *(doesn't know)*

At break, Jonny Garner confronts me and asks me to

JONNY: Stop kicking us boys in the balls!

GOOD GIRL: So I… kick him in the balls.

I kick balls with such relish that there is a school assembly warning against the dangers of kicking boys in the balls. But it's just a thing I do now. Exercising this bigness in me.

(Boombastic by Shaggy)

1997, We are twelve. Zoe has

ZOE: finally decided that I'll marry Damon Albarn and just have a *fling* with Liam Gallagher… he's just not marriage material at the end of the day.

GOOD GIRL: And Sarah has a new

SARAH: Guinea pig. Tootsie. Tootsie has a natural Mohawk. When my rabbit tried to have sex with her she weed in his face. I take her everywhere with me.

GOOD GIRL: Emergency conference at Laura's. Thick pink carpet, spread-eagled, legs in the air, knickers hanging off one foot, we crane to see our own fannies. Laura leads us in this exploration. With great gravity, she holds open her labia.

LAURA: Right. How's it going to fit in?

GOOD GIRL: This is a revelation. We haven't actually thought about this before.

SARAH: And what's all this extra frilly bit? It's weird.

ZOE: Well that's to protect the wee hole inn't it.

SARAH: I think the wee hole is your fanny hole Zoe.

GOOD GIRL: Yeah, I don't think I have a wee hole.

LAURA: Everyone has a wee hole dipstick.

GOOD GIRL: Silence while we continue our investigation. I catch Tootsie watching me from under the bed munching on a carrot.

(GG shrugs at Tootsie like "What is your problem?")

LAURA: What I want to know is, is it going to be painful?

ZOE: I think so. Yeah.

LAURA: I just don't understand how anything's actually meant to fit in here.

SARAH: No I can hardly get my finger in mine.

LAURA: Right.

GOOD GIRL: Craning to see all this is difficult to say the least. From this moment forth, during every wee, I use a compact mirror.

(Good Girl shuts the bathroom door behind her, locks it and sits on the loo with a mirror)

I still can't see 100% where the wee is coming from. And I'm not sure I actually have a "wee hole" when dad shouts up the stairs

DAD: Helen Sharman's arrived!

GOOD GIRL: I wee all over my hand. Fuck fuck fuck.

Do you know who she is? Helen Sharman? She was the first British astronaut to go into space. Not Tim Peake. Helen Sharman and she's our neighbour's sister. My dad goes crazy when he realises. What a perfect role model for his daughter! And she's at the bottom of our stairs. We shake hands and she says lots of encouraging things to me in a quiet, serious voice but I'm not listening. I'm just thinking about the fact I'm shaking hands with an astronaut. With wee on my hand. She's touched my wee... and space. *(Wow!)*

She gives me a signed photograph of herself with the words 'aim high' written underneath and I put stickers of moons and stars around the frame and hang it in pride of place between Michael Jackson and Henry VIII. That night Dad wraps an arm round my shoulders, turns me towards the window. It's a full moon with a little twinkling friend beside it.

DAD: Venus looks very fine tonight.

GOOD GIRL: That's my favourite star.

He'll love that, I grin up at him.

DAD: It's a planet love. Venus is a planet.

GOOD GIRL: I do not become an astronaut.

(Don't Stop Till You Get Enough by Michael Jackson)

Sally hits the ball hard and it looks like it's going to be a rounder but the ball is heading to my fielding area and I run to make an easy catch. *(GG crumples into tears)* When this sadness just hits me and I can't stop crying and there's absolutely no reason for it whatsoever. And now I've dropped the ball.

There's a problem. My edges are getting leaky. I start having these random crying fits. Full blown hurricane crying that is the precursor to panic attacks but it's the 90s, no one knows what the fuck is going on. What am I meant to do? Page someone? Everyone's too busy reading Garfield and eating Vienettas. The crying hits without warning. I'm in the changing room in C&A, a denim skirt half way up my legs when *(breaks down crying)*. I order a 99 from the ice-cream van man but when he turns back around he can't see me *(breaks down)* because I'm on the floor – howling. I cry when I'm happy, I cry when I'm sad.

I look at Laura, cool as a cucumber. I mean what is going on in there? I need to know if we are made of the same stuff.

GOOD GIRL: Laura, do you ever get so sad you could just disappear. Not like wanna kill yourself or anything but just… not exist anymore?

LAURA: No. Do you?!

GOOD GIRL: No. Of course not. I'm not a weirdo! *(smiling through gritted teeth)*

LAURA: OK…

GOOD GIRL: It's been a week so I try again.

Laura, do you ever get so happy you need to crack your ribs open just to give you space to feel it all?

LAURA: Oh my god why are you asking me that?

GOOD GIRL: Just checking you are not a mental case.

The crying fits get worse. Mr. Melgate is having a field day asking me

MR. MELGATE: Have you started your period yet?

GOOD GIRL: Which I haven't but eventually say

Yes, I have!

Because hopefully that'll stop him asking me. This backfires because now everyone thinks there's an actual woman in the class which there isn't but it doesn't stop me giving out advice anyway.

Periods? It's nothing to worry about, it just feels like... having a... painful...wee.

It becomes increasingly important to have my nails painted a bright colour. It's reassuring. This is where I end and where I begin.

(Mamma Mia by ABBA)

1999, We are 14. Sarah is

SARAH: Really concerned about the millennium bug.

GOOD GIRL: Zoe knows

ZOE: All the words to No Scrubs

GOOD GIRL: and I have an extensive collection of platform trainers.

Emergency conference at Laura's. Thick pink carpet.

LAURA: Right. So, who here has had the big O? *(She scans the room expectantly)* That's an orgasm.

GOOD GIRL: I have a coughing fit. I've inhaled a Skip. Sarah raises her hand like she's suddenly remembered an answer to a question in class.

SARAH: I think I have.

LAURA: You can't think you have, either you have or you haven't, it's as simple as that.

SARAH: Yes, then I have?

LAURA: Well if you have what does it feel like then?

SARAH: Erm, it's like *sharp* but at the same time like really *really* nice.

GOOD GIRL: Laura nods sagely and confirms that she too has had a "sharp but at the same time really *really* nice orgasm". Zoe and I look at each other. We've talked about this in private before. Apart from Swayze-ing we have not really… well, we've not touched ourselves. With any real skill. It's like we haven't been taught and it just hasn't come naturally to us. But now it looks like we've been left behind.

Mine feels like a tickle.

I lie.

Zoe backs me up. Because she's a legend.

ZOE: Yeah mine too, it makes me laugh, it doesn't hurt, not at all, not like yours.

GOOD GIRL: We all look each other in the eye taking stock. Unsure who is lying and who is telling the truth. How can we ever know what's going on in each other's bodies, really? How can we ever know for sure? Makes me feel sort of lonely.

Later, Laura smells my jim jams and says they smell like curry

LAURA: but not in a nice way.

We bring up the video player to watch supernatural teen horror *The Craft* undisturbed, and crawl into Laura's king size bed.

LAURA: Right, before we start – quick question. Would you ever sell your body for money?

GOOD GIRL: Erm, I don't know.

SARAH: Would you do it for a hundred pounds?

GOOD GIRL: Er...

LAURA: Would you do it for five hundred?

GOOD GIRL: ...Maybe. Yeah.

LAURA: *(long pause while Laura looks at everyone)*

That's *disgusting*. I'd never sell myself.

SARAH: Me neither.

LAURA: I'm priceless.

ZOE: Can we watch the film now?

GOOD GIRL: We watch *The Craft*, rewinding all the best scary sexy bits, followed by a witching practice. Sarah lays on the ground and we three kneel around her in pink candlelight, our fingertips pressed under her body. 'Light as a feather stiff as a board, light as a feather stiff as a board.' I feel my edges start to shudder and blur, and I feel as if I am seeping into Sarah and my finger tips are pressed against what must be Sarah's but are also now my ribs and she I feel… weightless.

LAURA: We've got to stop doing this girls, it's stupid.

GOOD GIRL: I look down at my fingers. They look all puckered. Like I've been in the bath too long.

(Voulez Vous by ABBA)

(GG finds several pieces of art with dick doodles on them)

The boys are drawing dicks on everything. Take your eye off any flat surface for a minute and a boy will have drawn a dick on it. Which is really annoying if it's like an art project.

Because you have to throw it away. Or incorporate a dick in it somehow.

It started off with your basic primitive dick and balls and evolved to include pubic hair, a bell-end, a hand, sometimes with sperm shooting out the end and for the most artistic, thick veins running up it. I rack my brains on how to how to respond to this new development from the boys.

(She sees a boy's book and starts drawing in it)

I start drawing vaginas on all their work. Which is quite complicated actually. But I get good at it. It's a guerrilla vagina attack. At first they don't know what they are, Nadeem is baffled.

NADEEM: What the fuck is that? Is that an ordinance survey? A hill gradation map?

GOOD GIRL: Unlike the cartoon cocks, my vaginas are very realistic.

This is anatomically correct actually.

THE BOYS: Is that what yours looks like? You should get that sorted out.

GOOD GIRL: I'm not worried that the boys think my vaginas are weird because I've seen three other vaginas up close. And let's just say, I'm pretty handy with a 3B pencil. Soft, for shading.

I'm in the art rooms sketching a particularly lovely goldfish, I love extending their fins into swirly fronds, when Nadeem walks over with his two new buddies Robbie and Pete. He drops an open magazine on top of my sketch. It's a double page spread of a lady, with the most perfect vagina I have ever seen.

NADEEM: That's what they should look like.

GOOD GIRL: I look down at this perfectly peachy pink thing in front of me. It's hairless, it's symmetrical, it's, it's just perfect and it looks nothing like mine. I can't tear my eyes away.

NADEEM: Not like a stuffed kabab!

GOOD GIRL: He rolls the magazine into his rucksack and they laugh themselves out the room.

On the bus, I draw faces in the condensation on the window *(draws smiley face, then sad face)*. But the image of an overstuffed pita won't go away, frilly layers of lamb dance in front of me.

HIGH-VIS MAN: Eh that fucking stinks.

GOOD GIRL: By the door, four men in high-vis vests are eyeing up a woman while insulting her dog.

It's one of those small wrinkly ones with a squished nose. She keeps her head down and gives it a little kick to get it off the bus. I watch them. Spread out. Hanging off the hand poles. My stop next. Press the button. Stand up. They look. Here we go. Walk towards them. Keep my eyes on the ground. Don't wanna draw attention to myself. But at the same time, no, stay proud. Stood in the middle of them. Waiting for the doors to open. Why aren't they opening? And it's like someone has left the gas on and lit a match because my insides go up in flames. My face is on fire. I catch the one in front of me smirking at the others behind me. Feel them scanning my body. Prickly electricity playing under the surface of my skin. If they say one word to me, I'm gonna– yeah, I'm gonna fight them. Doors open. Step out and… nothing. *(She looks back.)* They are laughing at me. And for the second time today I am wondering what is so funny about my body?!

I get home and announce to dad

When I grow up I'm going to be a man.

He nods and without looking away from the telly says

DAD: Oh yeah? There are operations for that.

(Beat It by Michael Jackson)

(GG looks around at the three girls sympathetically and gazes at the pillow in the middle of them. She whispers, respectfully)

GOOD GIRL: Tootsie is dying. She is lying on what Sarah calls 'her death pillow'. It's just a normal pillow. But there's a guinea-pig dying on it. A week ago she stopped eating.

SARAH: It's like she's on strike.

GOOD GIRL: I look at us four. Staring at this black unmoving mass. Willing it to live. Or die. Or just make up its mind and put Sarah out of her misery. When I know what I have to do. I know what I have to do, you know?

Wait here!

Tootsie almost falls off her death pillow.

I rummage around in my rucksack where I keep literally everything I could possibly need in case of an emergency. So, mainly packets of Twix. And hold up the pink candle like it's a trophy. They are not sure. Not sure at all. But I ignore them because I've got this feeling, this strong feeling in my belly that this is going to work. Because we –

Because we are magic. Sarah, you light the candle. Zoe – close the curtains. Everyone get in a circle.

We are transforming into a witches' coven.

Hold hands – oh Laura put on that Enya track. Close your eyes… Picture the candle.

I've no idea what I'm doing so I'm going to have to make this up.

The light is a healing pink. Imagine it is travelling into Tootsie.

I know it's nonsense, but at the same time it's kind of not you know? And they are into it.

The light is healing Tootsie. We three lady witches are heal/…

/and I feel Sarah's hand start to vibrate. She's giggling. She's trying not to but it means she makes little snorting sounds. Like a piglet. *(laughs)* And now, yep, we're all laughing. We are all absolutely howling with laughter and I think, ah, yeah, ha ha, this is, yeah this is love. We four are conjuring love real love. My love is so big it pours out of my palms and into Laura and Sarah and out my eyes and into Zoe and we howl and love and love and love.

Then Tootsie squeals. No word of a lie Tootsie, with one paw clawing meekly on death's door, squeals and it's like she is laughing too. We scream with delight. We can heal the sick and levitate each other with our fucking fingertips and our minds. I explode with love.

And that's when I bite Laura.

LAURA: What the fuck?!

(GG looks horrified at what she's done)

(Lay All Your Love on Me by ABBA)

MRS. HOG: Covalent bonds. Write this down.

GOOD GIRL: Laura three seats away is folding a note, ostentatiously.

She looks self-righteous. Tight-lipped. Oh fuck. She hands the note over to Sarah who reads it, nods and now she too has tight lips. Oh fuck oh fuck oh fuck.

MRS. HOG: The sharing of electrons between atoms is called a covalent bond, which holds the atoms together.

GOOD GIRL: Sarah hands the note over to Zoe who holds it in her fist, refusing to pass it on. I snatch it off her. Well it's for me after all, isn't it?

Laura's perfect handwriting 'I don't want you around me anymore. I don't want to be your friend.'

MRS. HOG: Atoms covalently bonded as a molecule are more stable than they were as separate atoms.

GOOD GIRL: Another note is passed rapidly down the line. I un-crumple it.

'You are too intense.'

There is a love heart over the 'I'.

Mrs. Hog sees me sat bolt upright, wet-faced, chin wobbling. Please don't say anything.

MRS. HOG: ...Oh GG.

GOOD GIRL: And I'm out of there. Running, half blind. The ball of pain pushing up against my skin, screaming in my head. *See, this is why you don't fit in.* Expanding. *You're a freak.*

And I'm stood in the middle of a street I don't recognise. Sight super sharp. Everything hyper real. Like a video game. My brain is tingling.

I have to make a choice, to survive. I don't want to feel anymore. I want to be cool as a cucumber. I have to be stronger than this thing inside me.

Through sheer will power, and the will of a teenage girl is strong, I harden every soft part of me, 'til I start to taste – yeah, metal? There's a click in my neck. That's interesting. I feel it in the back of my eyes and in my brain. Everything is straight lines. The burning ball is... quiet. Caged in this new *steel* in my belly. It's peaceful. I take a moment to contemplate. It's not immediate but by just a few degrees I'm set on a different trajectory to feeling... nothing. Numb.

My 14-year-old body and I stand in the middle of the street and I feel for the first time, in control.

PART II

(Ray of Light by Madonna)

(GG is having sex throughout this. It shouldn't be too distracting from her text. He's behind.)

GOOD GIRL: He's panting and calling out my name. He's shortened it and I think it's funny how he barely knows me and yet he's found a term of endearment for me no-one else has thought of before. His panting has turned to deep gasps now I think we're almost there. I'm not feeling much but I'm putting on a good show.

The physical sensation is akin to having your hand squeezed but not tenderly, it's more like being patted, or better, softly punched. It's not hurting. I'm numb. There's no connection. It's like I'm, well I'm just switched off.

But this nickname, well it's sweet and just for a moment I imagine being in love with him, and just for a moment something flickers on. And then off.

(She pulls up her pants and nods to him)

I never stay the night.

(Papa Don't Preach by Madonna)

ZOE: You're back you dirty stop out. I was worried about you.

GOOD GIRL: Why? Is yours still here?

ZOE: I kicked him out. It was disgusting. He had a cold he kept dripping all over me.

2006. We are 21. London is having a heatwave. Zoe and I do everything together other than she's down the road at the nursing college and I'm studying the highly practical degree of English Literature.

ZOE: Hurry up we're going for lunch.

GOOD GIRL: *(Does lipstick in mirror)* 'I'm tough, I'm ambitious, and I know exactly what I want. If that makes me a bitch, okay.'

That's not me. That's Madonna.

(Papa Don't Preach by Madonna)

Ow. Zoe kicks me under the table. She's sat between my two Uni buddies, on the right is

SAM: Sam. I've got floppy curtains like I'm in a 90s boyband and a billowing white shirt whose top four buttons have never been done up.

GOOD GIRL: There is no sexual tension between me and Sam. Unlike with my other male friends. You know that tension, where you could have sex at any point? It could happen, at any time.

And on the left,

AMERICAN FRANCES: American Frances. The works of Virginia Woolf are like my bible. So, coming to England has been – a pilgrimage.

GOOD GIRL: The Waitress asks me for the third time

WAITRESS: Have you decided…yet?

GOOD GIRL: …

I am a practised non-feeler. I've spent the last 7 years learning how not to care. Like I don't give a shit. But the annoying side effect is, when I check in with my gut feeling, like, do I want this? No response. Chronic indecision.

I've got a pob, that's a Posh Spice bob, because I told the hairdresser

Just do what you'd have, if you had my face.

I spend an hour in Sainsbury's deciding on a lemon. Unwaxed lemon? Waxed lemon? Unwaxed lemon? Waxed lemon?

When faced with any decision I personify the French sentiment of '*bof*'.

I'll just have what she's having.

But does it even matter what decision I make when the consequences of my decisions always make me feel – well… how will I feel if I shoplift this necklace? *Bof.* What about if I slap that man? *Bof.*

FRANCES: Try this bloody Mary GG, it's fantastic.

GOOD GIRL: *(GG takes the drink whilst talking to us)* I'm waiting for a tangible reaction to my actions but I'm not getting any so I travel at high speed exploring the endless boundaries of this numbness.

(Passes the drink back) That *is* good thanks.

Where are the walls? I'm like a scientist measuring cause and effect.

ZOE: I love the décor in here. It's sort of colonial inn't it.

GOOD GIRL: It's great isn't it?

I mean how many men do I have to sleep with before I actually feel something?

FRANCES: Can I have a coffee?

GOOD GIRL: Yeah, me too.

What about women? Strangers? Riskier but it feels like floating.

SAM: You women shouldn't drink so much caffeine it's not good for your reproductive systems.

GOOD GIRL: He's probably right, I won't drink mine.

I could walk through walls and not feel a thing, I feel invincible. But also a bit like a ghost.

Men suddenly think they get me.

SAM: The thing about you GG, is that you know what you want and you know how to get it and you don't care if it makes you a bitch.

GOOD GIRL: It drives me on.

(Unapologetic Bitch by Madonna)

Parties are the best at Sam's because he's got an eclectic CD collection.

Sam, can I borrow your laptop?

I can't speak French but da da da da lalaalalaa dong donk dong dun duuun. I'm not into Girl's Aloud but I love this bit. Makes me want to write something inspiring… on Facebook.

Sam is still logged on. *(She looks around)* Check his messages.

One from a lady. Renaissance poetry Karen, the one with a face like a slapped arse? I know that sounds mean but she does always have a miserable face. Like really though that is going to be a problem for her in life, you know what I mean?

'Why are you hanging out with that psycho-bitch GG' So, there we are. That's what people think of me.

I take Sam by the hand, pull him into his bedroom and try to have sex with him.

Like a psycho-bitch.

(Unapologetic Bitch by Madonna)

It's really late but I creep into Zoe's bed, lay my head on her chest. *(Inhales her)* Milky.

GOOD GIRL: *(Whispering)* Zoe, can I tell you something?

ZOE: What? What do you want?

GOOD GIRL: I don't feel much – anything – anymore. Do you get that? It's like there's a bubble around me yeah and nothing out there can like get in here. Do you know what I mean?

She rolls over and I see her shoulders are shaking and at first I think she's laughing at me but then I realize she's crying. And I know I should hold her, tell her that it's okay but as I say, I'm not feeling it, anything, you know?

(Body Shop by Madonna)

Every week I get a letter in the post from my dad. I can tell it's him by the double underlined address. Does he think that will help it get to its destination quicker? London. Line line. As if the postman thinks 'wowee it's a double underliner, I better deliver this!' Inside is some 'article of interest' that has been cut out and circled in blue biro. The only words written are 'Interesting!' or 'Of interest?' He used to get me a subscription until he came to visit and saw piles of unread newspapers being used as a coffee table.

He's circled Revamped National Army Museum to Feature Live Horse. And next to it 'Of interest?' I fold it, intending to read it – someday – and see on the back are the job adverts. I love looking at the job adverts. Imagining what I'll do when I'm a real grown up.

Sherlock Holmes walking tour guide. Mmm nah. Aquarium assistant. Ooo quite fun. Girls wanted for masked parties. £200-an-hour minimum. Experience preferred but not essential. Call Lucinda for details.

(Beat)

Fuck it. I call her.

She's got this warm, reassuring voice and I think I hear children in the background. Which is a bit weird when she asks me

LUCINDA: Do you do anal?

GOOD GIRL: But we laugh about it when I say

I don't know!

LUCINDA: You seem like a nice girl. I'll look after you.

GOOD GIRL: I didn't even know I needed looking after but this feels really nice.

LUCINDA: Just send me the photos that's a good girl.

GOOD GIRL: It's like morphine. I want to please this woman so bad and it feels good.

(Body Shop by Madonna)

(Holding a dildo) I'm not putting that inside me.

Zoe has just handed me a sparkly pink dildo in Ann Summers. *(beat)* Everyone is having orgasms. Loud orgasms that are made to be overhead. They scream EMPOWERMENT. But they are not real. At least I hope they're not real because mine aren't. When I tell Zoe this she frog-marches me here. To the Rampant Rabbit section.

GOOD GIRL: It's vile and it smells like My Little Pony ponies.

She takes me by the chin. She's very firm.

ZOE: Just try it.

GOOD GIRL: I buy a small, black, bullet. It's some sort of low-fi vibrator. I mean I'll just try the thing and get it over with.

The buzzing is very loud. It's embarrassing. Even though there's only me in my room, I'm embarrassed.

(She uses the vibrator uncertainly)

Nothing.

(Pause)

Nope.

(Pause)

Nuhuh.

I'm here for two hours.

This is pointless. Doesn't she know my body doesn't work like that? It's humiliating. My body has let me down. I've come to accept this. We have a relationship of tolerance. I'll feed it, take it for exercise and it'll keep working in a basic and efficient way for me.

It's just bits of skin and hair and nails and veins and synapses and muscle contractions and WOAH WOAH WOAH

My body is talking back to me. And it is a very serious conversation. I'm feeling connected in a way I've never felt before and it starts, yeah it's starting at the back of my head. Oh this is new.

It's, it's, yeah, it's like a very serious, yeah, a very serious Swayze? No it's a bit different. It's kind of more, erm, more heavyweight. It has depth, it's more complete. Oh, Toto we ain't in Kansas anymore. Hold on, ok, my sight is going now. I mean is this normal? And I'm seeing stars, yes actual stars. It's all systems go. Houston we have a solution! My brain is on fire and there's some sort of explosion that is going to happen in space and it's going to be hot and it's going to be prickly it's going to be really really really good, and pleasure, yes real pleasure shoots out. Boom! A bomb has gone off. In me. Is it possible that this, this body can produce pure joy? It's the realest thing I've ever felt. I'm overwhelmed with gratitude, for myself. *(She kisses her hands and arms)* Thank you. Thank you. Thank you.

Suddenly there is a battery shortage in the house.

Just a glimpse at a double A really gets me going. I'm taking them from remote controls, clocks, radios, anything that doesn't have a wire attached. I'm basically in a honeymoon period with my own vagina. I invest in a very fancy rechargeable little number. Zoe is relieved. Time has had to stand still for about a week. The clocks start working again.

I want to tell everyone about my new superpower. I have orgasms! I make them myself!

I do tell American Frances.

I don't mean to show off, but I do have rather nice orgasms, and I'm quite new to all of this so it's just nice to share it with another woman, you know?

FRANCES: Uhuh, how long does it take you?

GOOD GIRL: How long does it take me?

FRANCES: Yeah, does it take you a long time? It used to take me like forever, like 10 minutes but now I've got it down to like 2.

GOOD GIRL: 2 minutes?!

FRANCES: Yeah, but I've got a cousin who can come from just having her nipples brushed. So, 2 minutes is actually a long time.

GOOD GIRL: Shit.

I spend what American Frances must consider to be a mammoth amount of time trying to get faster, better, more efficient in what has essentially become a vaginal arms race until one day... snap. The communication stops. Numbness. In African American literature:

FRANCES: Hey GG, how are the orgasms going?

GOOD GIRL: Yeah fine thanks, down to thirty seconds.

FRANCES: You know what I love about you?

GOOD GIRL: No, what?

FRANCES: You're just living your life. It's fantastic. You don't care that people think you're a whore.

(Girl Gone Wild by Madonna)

I am naked. And Zoe is naked. And we have a digital camera. This is feminism in action.

ZOE: I mean they're our bodies aren't they? Why not turn our deeply unsatisfactory sexual experiences with lads into a capitalist venture?

GOOD GIRL: I know! It's mad we weren't doing this before.

We are trying to achieve the perfect sexy photo so underneath all the fun, there's an underlying atmosphere of stress. Zoe looks, I must admit, pretty hot in her pictures. I think it's her hair. But when I look at mine...

GOOD GIRL: Oh my God! I look like an overfed Victorian schoolboy!

ZOE: No you don't! *(reconsiders)* Anyway some people might be into that.

We send the photos to Lucinda and go out that night to celebrate. I wear my tightest bodycon dress which I've padded to give me a completely different body shape from my own. I am free to be whatever I want to be. A 34EE and a person of destiny.

(Bitch I'm Madonna by Madonna)

In South London we are standing in front of a non-descript sort of business hotel. It's not as glamourous as we'd hoped. I don't know what we were hoping.

Calling gut feeling. No response. In times of uncertainty I ask myself 'what would Madonna do?' If I don't have an answer to that I refer to the next best thing, 'I don't know what I'm doing but I'm going to damn well do it.' Geri Halliwell.

A pale young woman with a clipboard greets us at the entrance.

MELANIE: Hi I'm Melanie. Are you girls here for the party?

GOOD GIRL: Yeah. Is Lucinda here?

MELANIE: *(Laughs)* Oh, she doesn't come to these events.

GOOD GIRL: She pushes us into our dressing room, a disabled loo, and hands us these yellow velvet masks.

Yellow is not my colour...

But she's already leaving with her clipboard.

Zoe and I help each other with fine fabric and fiddly attachments twisted on our thighs. Her fingers are cold. I feel looked after. I smile down at her and she smiles up at me. Her eyes are such a lovely chestnut brown.

But I am not sure that they are smiling.

It's basically a pimped-up conference lounge. *I don't know what I'm doing but I'm going to damn well do it.* Men sat around low tables.

Oh my God are we are actually doing this? I shuffle off to a corner pulling Zoe with me

ZOE: Chill out.

GOOD GIRL: and bump into – Foliage. Lovely tendrils in pots on copper stands. Like a wedding. I rub a waxy leaf between my fingers. Cut my nail in. Smells clean.

Two men are watching us. One in a stripy suit, the other in navy. *(GG quietly screams in excitement and fear with Zoe)*

Stripy beckons us over with a finger. Zoe and I look at each other. Squeeze each other's arms. *What would Madonna do?*

ZOE: What?

GOOD GIRL: Nothing.

We follow them down a corridor – *what is this place?* – to a room.

Stripy takes Zoe to a zebra print sofa and I look away them to give them I don't know, privacy or something, and Navy and I go into a bedroom.

When it happens, the service I'm here to perform. I know something's very wrong.

We're having sex and it's fine, it's numbness

like normal until... it's not. My body has decided to wake up and I'm feeling... yeah, I'm feeling connected. And the steel in my belly must be disintegrating because I'm feeling horror, and also joy. Horror that maybe... is it... am I enjoying this? Or am I enjoying being able to feel horror again? There is an overwhelming surging of emotion that is fucking familiar. Hello old friend. The burning ball is threatening to explode my body and my gut feeling is giving me a very clear message that I need to stop this now. But I'm here to do a job, I don't want to cause a scene. I don't want to disappoint Lucinda. I'm her girl. So I have to see this through. One thing is certain. If I have to do this again tonight, which inevitably I will, there'll be nothing left of me. I'll be an empty bag of skin on the floor.

(Pause)

He's finished and I try to be polite but I can barely stand I feel like I've no bones, I need to leave now. Zoe's in the corridor looking down at her mask.

ZOE: It's not the same. It's not the same as with the lads.

GOOD GIRL: We don't change just wrap our coats around us and smiling at Melanie, leave.

ZOE: This is your fault. You. You got us into this. You happy?

GOOD GIRL: We receive a text at the same time. Lucinda. Confusingly she says I'm not your mother followed by a torrent of texts. We're not going to get paid. Unless we do another job. Then we'll get paid for half this job as well as for that job.

So not bad really. Not a complete waste then.

ZOE: There is something wrong with you, you know.

GOOD GIRL: Have you ever seen it when someone gets really, really angry and their actual eyes change? Have you? When their eyes change in front of you? Like they belong to someone else. Or they are being possessed for a moment. The word grave pops into my head. Grave.

She tells me that I'm broken. I'm poison. She doesn't want to see me anymore. She needs space. From me. *(beat)* She's gone.

In my room, I cry for the first time in 7 years. I can't stop the feelings from coming, shame, anger, love rip through my body and it's more than my chest can take. I punch the sky and parts of me shoot out of my fingertips and fracture in the air like dust and matter and particles of me, I am no more than sound and light for I have no body anymore.

(Beat)

I take out my contact lenses, rub them between my fingertips until they tear and disintegrate. I never want to look through those again. Everything is blurry, like a new born fucking baby.

(Knowing Me, Knowing You by Abba)

2018?! *(How did we get here already/ What? /Such a long time!)*

I'm.../ we don't.../ I still.../ It's...

(Cues the music again and listens for a moment and regains strength)

I can tell how shitty I've been feeling by how much ABBA it takes to make me feel normal again. The ABBA Gold album is the best litmus test. If by Super Trouper I'm not tapping my foot, I can safely say it's been a bad day. Sometimes it takes until Chiquitita. And I don't even like that one very much. If it's a mild shittiness I can usually shake it with a couple of Michael Jacksons. Bad. Dirty Diana. But for the worst days: ABBA. At first it feels jarring. You don't want to listen to upbeat 70s pop when you feel like your insides are chewed up and you're doing everything you can not to scream into a pillow but after a few bars… or when the beat really kicks in.

(A few bars of Chiquitita play over the next part of text here – from 4.40 into the track, when it really kicks in – and we see GG leaving herself, playing the drums, dancing, it's free and strong)

I've discovered this is quite useful in times of extreme emotion. It allows me to exercise enormity of feeling without laying waste to my life.

(A sigh)

I still want to be a good girl. I like being all tucked in, bed sheets pulled up to my chin, arms folded on my chest, so good. I like it even better when I wake up and I haven't even moved from that position. I've just stayed still all night, like a vampire. It means I must have been very peaceful, internally, you know? Because good girls are neat. They have neat little emotions and tidy little vaginas and I don't have either of those. Particularly.

This is for the people who burst at the seams. Who feel like freaks because you live intensely, painfully, impossibly. You are not alone. That alive ball that swirls in your chest is your superpower. Big feelings are your thing. No more squashing them down until they become bad blood in our own bodies. Let's channel them like electricity (pew, pew). I want to live in a vivid, feeling world. No more apologies when I'm told I'm too much and yet always somehow never enough. No more apologies for my rage, my love or my shame. It's how I know I'm alive.

The End.